THE HOUR OF THE FURNACES

Also by Renny Golden

Oscar Romero
(with Marie Dennis and Scott Wright)

Disposable Children: America's Child Welfare System

The Hour of the Poor, the Hour of Women: Salvadoran Women Speak

Sanctuary: The New Underground Railroad
(with Michael McConnell)

Dangerous Memories: Invasion and Resistance Since 1492
(with Michael McConnell and Cinny Poppin)

The Hour
of the
Furnaces

poems by

Renny Golden

Mid-List Press
Minneapolis

Published by Mid-List Press
4324 12th Avenue South Minneapolis, Minnesota 55407-3218
Website: www.midlist.org.

Manufactured in the United States of America

First printing: March 2000

Library of Congress Catalog Number: 00-131647

Acknowledgments for previously published poems: "Accompaniment" in *International Quarterly;* "Artist's Daughter" in *Freedom's Just Another Word* (Crete, Illinois: Outrider Press, 1998) and *Americas Review;* "Cotton Pickers of Chinandega" in *Calyx, Sing, Heavenly Muse,* and *Naming the Daytime Moon* (Chicago: Feminist Writers Guild, 1987); "Last Desire" in *Sojourners;* "Tatu" in *Anthology of Midwestern Poetry.*

CONTENTS

FOREWORD

What is to become of us?

We set upon the earth the iron foot of the warrior. First the foot, then the thigh, the greed, the quick lunge, the weaponry, the invasion. There follows the 'first death,' inevitably of the innocent. But less taken in account is the 'second death' of which scripture warns—that of the booty, loot, sour memories, addiction to violence, contempt for life. It is we who live in this Land of Second Death.

I shake my head in disbelief and belief. I feel the awful force of events we've been cursed and blessed to witness in this lifetime of blood and betrayal. And then Renny Golden's poems whisper tenderly: "Let's have the courage to take a second look, or a third; and then, having done that, let's show some mercy toward ourselves."

That Golden speaks for the dead, and better still, lets the dead speak for themselves, seems to me the supreme requiem, the dignity denied, the second life after the horrid 'second death.' Her poetry is an act of compassion—toward us. It is time, time long past, that our poets help raise from death the Land of the Second Death, its one-eyed giants, its technological dwarfs.

So the poet borrows and brings home the stories of those others who have withstood our self-destroyed warrior souls, who, under the warrior's heel, have taught the warrior (were we not deaf, blind, halt, dumb) a better way to walk the earth.

This, it seems to me, is Golden's gift to us. The nuns, the cotton pickers, the Jesuits, the madres, the catechists—such lives and deaths are hardly indigenous to the Land of the Second Death. Their memories, their stories must somehow, against all odds, reach us.

DAN BERRIGAN

Now is the hour of the furnaces
only light should be seen.

—Jose Marti

INTRODUCTION

Too often in revolutionary wars, it is the selfless—those who defend the powerless, who risk their lives for others, who give up their food, water, and shelter so that others might be fed and sheltered—who are the first to die. Unfortunately, those who are the first to die are often the first to be forgotten. This book remembers, and, in doing so, takes us to a place of such profound risk that everything, everything, must be called into question. "What did you do," asks the slain Guatemalan poet, Otto Rene Castillo, "when the poor burned out like a dying flame?"

This collection of poems aspires to be both poetry and social history. The voices in these poems—clergy, human rights workers, peasants, and guerrillas caught up in the wars that plagued Central America over the last couple of decades—speak from Salvadoran graves, from Guatemalan highlands, from dank jails, from primitive hide-outs, from ghost towns, from country churches. The poems are divided into two main sections: martyr poems and peasant poems. Each martyr and each peasant is presented first in a brief prose account, then in a poem.

I began writing these poems over fourteen years ago when I first went to El Salvador. Urged by Salvadoran refugees in sanctuary in Chicago to see "the face of war" personally, I began to travel to El Salvador in 1985, and have continued to visit the country almost every year since. Being with the Salvadoran people as they faced their "hour of the furnaces" changed my life. Their hope and ingenuity astonished me. I remember speaking with members of the community of peasant catechist Brigido Sanchez, who was being held and tortured by the Salvadoran military. The peasants knew exactly what Sanchez was experiencing: being shocked, beaten, forced to squat for hours at a time. They could not afford despair. Their one prayer: *Hold out, Brigido, hold out!* He did. Unlike so many others, he returned to the community. His strength, he said, came from knowing the community was there for him. The Salvadorans' sense of being a people, of the power of *comunidad*, was miraculous to me, immersed as I was in a culture of individualism.

This sense of *comunidad* derives from the people's long history of conquest and the theft of their land. The peasants' struggles in Central America

1

have always been about land. To this day, to advocate for true land reform in El Salvador or Guatemala is to risk being branded a subversive.

In 1977, when Oscar Romero was installed as Archbishop of San Salvador, fourteen Salvadoran families controlled sixty percent of the arable land. The struggle for land dates to the Spanish conquest and the decision of the ruling elite in 1881 to abolish indigenous communal land rights in order to allow the coffee barons to consolidate their holdings. The process of land theft continued until 1932, when the indigenous populations rose up to challenge the coffee barons' protectors—the Salvadoran military. In what Salvadorans refer to as "the Massacre," the army responded to the challenge by killing more that thirty thousand people in a month. The insurrection against the coffee barons was spearheaded by Farabundo Marti, a Marxist, and by Felician Ama, a religious leader of the Indian masses. The rebellion was doomed from the start. The peasants had centuries of rage in their hearts but only machetes in their hands.

By 1961, twelve percent of the peasants were landless; by 1971 thirty percent were landless; and by 1980 an estimated sixty-five percent were landless.

When the cry for land was heard again in the late 1970s, the large plantation owners and their right-wing paramilitary forces attacked the farmers who were attempting to organize cooperatives in the rural areas and the priests, nuns and human rights workers who defended the poor majority. Right-wing graffiti in San Salvador read: "Be a patriot, kill a priest."

Within weeks after Romero was elected in 1977, Father Rutilio Grande was killed. Months later almost two hundred campesinos in Rutilio Grande's area were murdered by the military and paramilitary, and Father Octavio Ortiz was killed with four students in the capitol. A scorched-earth policy drove thousands of peasants into the city or across borders into surrounding countries.

Although the Salvadoran army insisted their war was directed at the Farabundo Marti Liberation Forces (FMLM) guerrilla opposition, they were unable to "catch" the elusive guerrillas. They then sought to cut off the guerilla's support, which the military identified as ninety percent of the population. By 1980 search-and-destroy patrols were operating throughout the countryside. To demoralize and terrify civilians into submission, the military not only killed, they mutilated—skinning victims alive, slitting their throats, beheading them, tearing unborn children from their dead mothers' wombs.

Oscar Romero begged the United States to cease sending military or economic aid to El Salvador because, as he wrote to President Jimmy Carter, "it is used to repress our people." But the aid, amounting to 1.5 million dollars per day for twelve years did not cease until the 1990s when a United Nations Truth Commission issued a report revealing that the U.S. had backed a "murderous" army. Alone, wielding the maligned authority of his office, Romero did the only thing he could. He accompanied his people through the inferno of war. He called the act of walking at the side of the poor masses "accompanimiento." He confronted both his fellow bishops (all of whom, except Rivera y Damas, had tacitly supported the army), as well as the Salvadoran military, by publicly demanding that the repression cease. On March 24, 1980, he was assassinated.

The repression continued. Six hundred people, mostly women and children, were massacred at Sumpul River as they tried to cross into Honduras in flight from the military; one thousand peasants were killed in an intensive bombardment of the village of El Mozote in 1981. Years later the killings were unabated. In November 1989, six Jesuits and two women who worked with the Jesuits were slaughtered.

In 1991 the Salvadoran military and the FMLN negotiated a peace. Fearful that the negotiations would break down if they insisted on comprehensive land reform, the FMLN accepted peace accords that left many landless. Today, after so much bloodshed—eighty thousand killed, one million exiled, in a country of only five and a half million people—the situation for the poor majority remains essentially the same. One out of four Salvadoran children dies of a curable illness before reaching the age of five, and the average family makes four hundred dollars per year.

The Guatemalan military was just as ruthless during the 1980s. Over four hundred Mayan towns were incinerated and thousands were butchered. The Mayan people, who made up sixty percent of Guatemala's population, were targeted for elimination because they dared to resist land control policies that were starving them on lands they had cultivated for thousands of years. Since the 1954 CIA-backed overthrow of the first democratically elected civilian president of Guatemala, Jacobo Arbenz, the Guatemalan military has killed over 100,000 people. Even though peace accords were signed in 1995, Archbishop Gerardi Condera was assassinated after presenting the REMHI report in 1998. The report, based on the testimony of over three thousand people, found that the Guatemalan military had been responsible for over ninety percent of the killings during the war years of the 1980s and early 1990s.

Knowing this sorrowful history, one expects to find a defeated people. But Central Americans have made a critical historical decision to resist death and to struggle for life—or, at least, for the life of future generations. Their resistance has cost them dearly. And for what, some ask, when our children still have worms and babies die early? But even among those who question the struggle, the martyrs and the peasants who did not count their lives above others remain a memory they wield against the men with guns.

So here are the stories of these heroes and heroines, some well known, others not so well known. In the spirit of Central American liberation practice, the reader can whisper or shout *¡Presente!* as each life is presented.

THE MARTYR POEMS

LAURA LOPEZ

*It is time to go forward, Carmelo. There are moments when the
courage of men and women must become the feeling Jesus had
knowing he was going to die for the people.*

—Laura Lopez

LAURA LOPEZ was the people's "Bishop" because she was all that they had. No
priest had baptized a baby, blessed a wedding, or said the words of
Eucharist for years on the Guazapa volcano in El Salvador. No priest would
dare. Because the Salvadoran military considered Guazapa a haven for
guerrillas, anyone who ministered to the people was targeted by the armed
forces. Laura became one of the first casualties of the low-intensity conflict
when she was "cut down by flying bullets" on April 24, 1985.

In 1981, under the influence of Sister Ana, a pastoral team leader in
Laura's canton, Laura had decided to leave the relative safety of San
Geronimo to journey to Guazapa with her five children to live as a pastoral
worker. Once in Guazapa, she quickly became immersed in the lives of the
campesino poor.

When the air war began in 1985, Laura was determined to document
the indiscriminate bombing of civilians. Each time planes droned over-
head, she rushed for a camera and tape recorder. She sent communiques to
the International Red Cross and letters to the Christian churches and the
international press, noting carefully the number of bombs dropped, rock-
ets launched, and medios of sorghum, corn, beans, and sugar cane
destroyed. She also recorded the names of the families who suffered losses
and the numbers of compañeros captured or disappeared.

On March 9, 1985, the day after two A-37 bombers had flown over
Mirandilla and El Zopote dropping bombs, she wrote:

*All of us are hidden in a bomb shelter because we are well aware
that their bullets are waiting for us ... We are trying to defend our
lives, although we can no longer defend our huts or belongings.*

The bombing of the Guazapa villages intensified during Holy Week.

On Good Friday Laura gave this homily to her terrorized flock:

The martyr's cross has been placed on our shoulders... Our people
are tormented by our enemies ... but it has to be done. The word of
God has to be made a reality ... Our people have decided to end
this way of the cross but the final triumph is still down the line ...
We will not wait for people from other countries to show us what
has to be done. We are Christians and we know what we have to do.
But first we must sacrifice and make a serious decision to do so.

On April 16, Laura met with all the pastoral workers in Guazapa. They
were exhausted. A week before her death she wrote:

Despite our fatigue, after making an escape from an invading army,
we give thanks to God for protecting us. The work of the base
communities must continue because, if it were otherwise, what
would become of us?

The shelling continued. The people were on the run almost constantly
now. One of the targets was the village of Consolacion, Laura's base village.
As the bombs closed in, Laura fled with others into a tatu, or underground
shelter. When a family with children couldn't fit into the overcrowded hide-
out, Laura and her thirteen-year-old daughter gave up their space. Above
ground, they ran into the cane fields of Valle Verde, trying to outrun the
ground patrols. By three p.m., they were surrounded. The scorched cane
fields of Valle Verde were the end of Laura's journey.

TENDERNESS THAT HELD

1

The survivors have returned to
Guazapa volcano to remember.
They hold the wrinkled photo of you,
Laura, walking past a green wall of
pacun and eucalyptus, your face
a luminous fist opening, disarmed.
It is Sunday, wind stirs
in the maquilishaut groves.
Everything opens out
like a heart.

2

On Guazapa they seek your voice.
But rocks are not sea shells;
they whisper nothing, hold nothing.
Here, where the land received you,
weeds and wildrose
twist into an open field.
A village dog heaves itself onto
a patch of shade, whimpers.
He saw it all,
whatever animals see,
their minds pacific,
without memory or history,
except the trigger of sounds;
Julia and Ramon's names
called over and over
between the blows of a hundred
hammers exploding their frail shacks,
smashing cages, fences, corrugated roofs.
Their mother's voice pleading
across the milpa: "Julia, Ramon."
Until there was only silence

enveloping Guazapa.
The dogs remember fire.
The people, Laura.

3

You promised an exceptional tenderness
that held; a promise faced years ago
in San Geronimo when you asked Sister Ana,
"Up to what point must we give ourselves?"
It was not Ana who turned her eyes
toward the volcano. It was your eyes
leaving the ordinary hold of
troughs, corn bins, a green bean row,
the sight of your children startling
chickens that flap wildly in the dust.
Your eyes, cherishing a world you
would leave, an infant you would carry up
Guazapa's side, climbing alone
with five children, each lugging
their possessions: a plastic poncho,
one blanket, two books, pencils,
hammocks, pans, candles, seed;
their backs streaked with sweat.

4

Your oldest boy announced
when he was fifteen,
"Mama, I'm going up further,
to join the muchachos."
That grave son, trembling, resolute,
"I want to defend the poor," he said,
repeating you, repeating the only
choice he could imagine.
These were Guazapa's messiahs,
a boy, a widow.

5

The people ordained you "Bishop."
No ecclesiastic noticed,
a housewife teaching
catechism to illiterates.
As for sacramental authority,
what you had was packed
in your knapsack:
bread, alcohol for wounds,
sacramental oils, a few coins.

6

You climbed from village to village
pulling your exuberant
shadow over rutted paths.
Peasants in candlelight, gathered
amid tins of wild gajardo, spikenard,
a rage of singing, each hand tightening
in another's like a fist on a gun.
You are their priest, taking the shy,
toothless faces of mothers in your hands,
invoking the proclamation:
"You are the bread of our lives."
Nothing, not the tortured back of Pablo,
not the swollen body of Mario
who gave no names,
not holding that wrinkled baby
too weak to cry,
not Carmelo who begged
to teach in the impossible zones,
not the body of Monsignor,
a burst wine skin,
not Rio Sumpul—nothing
has ever proven you wrong,
nothing.

7

It is three o'clock,
the pink mouths of veranera buds
open above doomed fields,
the world ticking toward resurrection.

> Your daughter said:
> "We gave our space in the tatu
> for another family"

Then you are pastor,
your congregation zigzagging
in the whiz of tracking bullets.
Old Don Pedro lurches, his
fluttering hand orders you forward,
as his breath collapses. You take
his hand, priming speed, oxygen.
It's no use. He slips down
delicate as a cocoon.

You run unfettered, behind
your daughter who pummels through weeds,
and drops back to your side,
again and again.

Then you feel it, a snap of muscle,
fire in your thigh pushing out blood.

> "Mama tried to get up
> after the first shot.
> Another bullet hit her spine
> and she did not rise.
> Only the knapsack …
> She gave me the knapsack.
> 'Adelante!' my mama said,
> 'Adelante!'"

8

On the path ahead your child
finds six-year-old Carlos
shot in the testicles,
a puppy whimpering
in the dumb voice of helplessness.
Now your child improvises:
she is you,
she is a mother,
she is the church
she is thirteen years old.

"Come Carlos, I must carry you.
The soldiers are closing in."

A child carries
a wounded child,
small figures
stumble through a night
of laurel trees and blood.
Three days hiding:
this ravine, that field,
Carlos's thirst, the soldiers,
muddy boots she could touch,
crouched there, muffling Carlos's cries.
Carlos remembers everything,
dreams of guis birds that fly
up Guazapa and never return.

9

Carlos and his father
return to Valleverde to dig your grave.

The child says:
"It took us a week
to find Mama.

We wore bandannas
for the stench."
Where you fell
there is nothing, stones.
Sheaves of dust lift against
pochote and hog-plum trees.

10

After your death,
your children lived in the city,
watched Guazapa drifting above
the barrio's tin shacks
waiting near the stars,
its bashed shoulders, flocks
of zensontle picking its wounds.
Up there your man-child
walked the volcano's back,
a coyote familiar with night.
In April, 1989, the month
you, Bishop of Guazapa, fell,
your son was killed.

11

That is the month your oldest daughter
packed your knapsack, kissed
her sisters, and walked
toward Guazapa.
"Adelante!" she told them
and left.

STANLEY ROTHER, a farm boy from Oklahoma, was sent as a priest missionary to Santiago de Atitlan, Guatemala, in 1968. For twelve years, he worked among the Tzutihilm who harvest the steep mountainside surrounding Lake Atitlan. He collaborated in developing agricultural cooperatives and a health project that reduced infant mortality from fifty to twenty percent.

In 1981, faced with death threats following the murder of one of his catechists, he returned to the United States. Within months, however, he returned to Santiago Atitlan, telling his family he would rather die than abandon his people. He moved his sleeping quarters to a room over the church to evade surveillance by the death squads. On the night of July 28, 1981, however, a death squad broke into his room. Aware that captured victims were tortured until they give names, Rother physically resisted, demanding that the intruders kill him immediately.

Visitors to Atitlan can still see the bullet holes in the room. After his death, eight thousand Indians stood silently in the church plaza, refusing to be dispersed. The Indians buried Rother's heart under the altar at the church of Santiago de Atitlan.

In the following poem, the priest's catechist tells of Rother's last moments when the death squad came for him.

THE GRINGO'S HEART

They've come, Padre,
hitting our door in echoes,
each blow a stutter of death.
They've trampled our flowers.
Now their fragrant boots
pound up the stairs for you.
They drag me, hands tied, to your room.
Still, I don't believe them.
Not a gringo, a priest, not yet.
I didn't believe you, either.
A gospel for those who suffer,
why not from them?
No offense, what do you know?
Grandson of farmers who lost their land
when the dust rose against them
like a wall of sea, bleaching
crops and cattle.
Your people did not pull
their children's incinerated bodies from
ashes or mass graves.

They are drawing their weapons right now.

> "Come out priest, or we
> kill this catechist."

Ha! They think you are the source of our
stubbornness, these Mayans who hate themselves,
who sell prophecy for tortillas.

Now, Padre, break through
the window, rapido!
My mouth fills with blood
from blows I don't feel.

The eye of my mind,
watches you leap across
the church roof, down sacristy steps
swallowed into a labyrinth
these wolves cannot sniff.
Run, Conchito, run!

But it is me you will save,
the doe circling away from her young,
positioning herself in the crossfire.
So your door opens
light spilling away, deliberate.

                    "Let him go,"
                    you plead.

Their dark rush fills that room,
squeezing light into columns of shadow,
your face alone still lit.
In that moment we both see your future.
Under torture everyone gives names.
Oh, priest, your big hands tremble.
You turn now to your last congregation,
as if to bless but instead give orders:

                    "Kill me now.
                    Kill me here."

You do not lift your arms, do not kneel,
nothing after the clap of your voice.
They fired again and again, obedient
as if you held their hands.

The next morning, no bells,
only feet drumming down the volcano's
sides, lightly, quietly,
as if it might be awakened.

Thousands more walking up
from Atitlan's lake villages—
red, yellow, fuchsia headdress
bobbing in rivers of light—
filling the church plaza,
silent as thieves or witnesses
who will not testify,
who will not leave the murder scene.

When the colonels arrive,
a path rustles open
through a rain of dark faces
then swallows, closing.
The colonels walk quickly, announce:

> "We'll make arrangements,
> fly the body to Oklahoma,
> to his parents."

A cofradia leader moves forward,
behind him centuries of silence,
before him, thousands of voices
held, like a breath, like a heart stopped.

> "No," he says,
> "The priest belongs to us."

For days there are phone calls, entreaties.
When I rise to speak, our leaders listen
because I knew you best.

"Keep his heart," I say,
"send Stanley back to Oklahoma."
Through a translator I ask your mother's permission.
When she cries, I add,
"The heart that broke for us."

HERBERT ERNESTO ANAYA

HERBERT ERNESTO ANAYA was president of the non-governmental Human Rights Commission of El Salvador (CDHES), which documented human rights abuses and prepared reports for international human rights agencies. He was gunned down by two assassins as he waited to take his children to school on the morning of October 26, 1987. Anaya was the seventh leader of CDHES to be murdered or disappeared.

A frequent visitor to open graves, morgues, and prisons, Anaya himself was imprisoned for several months before his murder. While imprisoned, he documented further human rights abuses. After his release from prison, his life was publicly threatened. He told his father he knew he would be killed.

Anaya's funeral was an occasion for the people to reclaim the streets of San Salvador. After the brutal massacres in the streets and attacks on popular organizations in the early 1980s, few Salvadorans had dared to gather in public. Forbidden to attend Anaya's funeral, however, thousands defied the military by following his coffin to the cemetery through streets flanked by armed soldiers.

In that room
photos of headless torsos,
a diagram explaining how the capucha
is placed over the head,
how breath collapses
inside the rubber mask.
Photos of kids, in their one school shirt,
their disappearance dates.
This is where you worked,
taking coffee and pupusas
with survivors and the dead.

How you must have
hated that room,
its terrible lists,
typing stacks of reports
that would turn to dust.

While others sought relief
in the countryside,
filling their lungs
with the fragrance of myrtle,
you wore a bandanna over
your mouth and nose,
digging for corpses—
peasants who took
loss and fury with them;
students who sobbed
to empty rooms,
hugging bashed ribs,
whispering, *nunca, nunca.*
The body is a mask,
you told yourself.
It hides the true self.

But the tender parts
lay there, and you would,
if you could, make the
bones and sinews
remember their sacred order.

What do they have
on me? you worried,
                        not death,
                        not torture,
                        not betrayal.
These things were familiar.
                        my children ...

and the list would stop.
You'd try to repeat,
finger the beads of your fear,
wanting your wife to take the children
to your aunt in Honduras.
But she wouldn't leave you.
Every morning you said,
Ninas de mi cariño—
this kiss is all you'll ever have,
all anyone ever has.

At times, unable to continue,
you brought the bruise
of your heart to the people,
riding the bus to the city's
edge, past barefoot
forty-year-old farmers
selling shoelaces and chicklets
while their scorched fields
held the secret of bodies;
then further out to railroad tracks
where your people ate

nuts and garbage
when the maize bin emptied.

After you fell,
they rose, Herbert,
emptying casitas of mud and plastic;
the city's margins, pressured by
their gasp of life, burst.
They filled the streets
as if they saw you those nights
weeping, filled with tenderness.
They called themselves:
Land, Bread, Work, and Liberty,
thousands barricading the streets
as if it were 1981, battling
the Guardia with their hands.

They rose up, Herbert,
those who were afraid,
those who were half dead,
those who were defeated,
they rose, Herbert,
they rose up.

MAURA CLARK

*The poor really strip you, pull you, challenge you, evangelize you,
show you God.*

—Sister Maura Clark

MAURA CLARK grew up in an Irish working-class family in Queens, New York. After entering the Maryknoll Order, she was assigned to Nicaragua in 1959, where she worked in the countryside in the village of Siuna and later in the poor barrios outside Managua. When a Maryknoll friend was drowned in El Salvador in 1980, Clark chose to take her place.

Faced with death threats and the rapidly increasing killings of campesinos, Maura Clark and her companion Sister Ita Ford flew to a Maryknoll sister's retreat in Nicaragua to decide if they should remain in El Salvador. On December 2, 1980, at peace with their decision to remain with the Salvadoran refugee community, they flew back to Salvador where they were picked up at the airport by Sister Dorothy Mazel and Jean Donovan. Their van was followed and intercepted by security forces. On a desolate road off the highway they were raped and assassinated. U.S. Ambassador Robert White implicated the Salvadoran High Command. The soldiers held responsible have kept silent for years, fearing their own death if they testified against superior officers.

When, in 1998, one of the soldiers was released from prison, he confessed that he had been ordered by ranking officers to kill the women. This confession, he said, was for him a death sentence, even in the "peaceful" period of the 1990s.

LETTER TO MARYKNOLL

There was no way to imagine this
thirty-five years ago when I walked
away from Pa, from Queens.
What I have of eighteen years
in Nicaragua is:
a habit of surrendering.

Tonight I will hold a four-year-old
while bombs rattle this casita.
Luis will cry, "Mama, oh Mama,"
and I will ask him, the others,
to sing the little chicken song.
They will smile numbly, and,
because they are peasants who treat
terror without the respect it deserves,
and kindness with audacious hunger,
they will sing the little chicken song,
clapping their trembling hands louder
if explosions thump our floor boards.

> *Pollita chiquitita, pollita chiquitita.*

Our medicines sit at a checkpoint
near El Paraiso, antibiotics that
could have saved Elena's baby.
Ita argues with them, her voice
thick with constraint,
the force of ocean pounding
in her pulse.

I know the Irish have tempers.
I never did. This is my rage.
Pa was IRA seventy years ago.
I won't say it publicly:

Sure she sympathizes with terrorists,
look at her old man.
I like Jorge, the FMLN commandante,
when he forgets to be intense.
He says we both have vows of fidelity.

The children's eyes seek
protection we can't give.
The ordinary hum of cicadas
lulling the stillness cannot
ease this night's terror.
The children sing Alleluia to the dark.
Alleluia before gun rattle,
Alleluia when a small shadow tiptoes
from the window, whispering:
"Sister, it is over for tonight."

What I have to give and take from this world is
one voice speaking with children who've seen
the dull, infinite stare of corpses.
What I know is that these bones
that once were children, hide something
the world cannot imagine.

Tonight, their small hands take ours,
an act of trust none of us deserve.
I have never felt this fragile.
I have never felt this powerful.
If my voice falls silent,
if this Irish heart stops,
bury it here with children whose singing
burned a hole in the engulfing fire.

OCTAVIO ORTIZ

At the end of your life you shall be judged by your love … How lovely it is to see a poor priest who renounced all, living with the simplicity of a field hand.
                          —Oscar Romero, at the funeral of Octavio Ortiz

OCTAVIO ORTIZ and four teenage members of his parish pastoral team were killed in the early dawn of January 20, 1979, when the National Guard broke into the Jesuit center, El Despertar, where the priest and the teenagers were making a retreat. After killing Ortiz, the soldiers rolled a tank over his body.

The parishioners of Ortiz's church, San Francisco Mejicanos, buried him behind the altar. During the war years, the parishioners celebrated a mass on the anniversary of his death as an act of resistance.

THE LAST TWO QUESTIONS

Guerrillas have blown power lines,
so the people burn candles,
as if the moment begged
a sudden loss of light,
the war, a renewal of
promises to the dead.
Twilight drenches the church,
the curves of their backs
in salmon light.
Octavio! Presente!

It's been thirteen years since
they cradled him through the streets,
hundreds behind the coffin,
drunk with rage or faith,
rocking insolently past the Guardia,
past the Jeep Cherokee's dark mirrors,
to lay down their priest.

Years since his last
retreat with pastoral leaders,
the youth he called
our future, our heart.
The night before he died, Octavio gave
two questions for the morning:
"What does it mean to give
liberty to the oppressed?"
"What does it mean to give
sight to the blind?"

Each question, a meditation that
chastened the body's longing to flee.
"Fear is natural," the priest said.
"So is love," they'd answered—

boys, idealists walking like firewalkers
through their burning country.
Even when soldiers kicked in the doors,
three rows of rifle muzzles
lifted into position,
a tank rumbling through
the retreat center gate,
they only looked for Octavio's eyes.

The blasts threw them against the wall
opened dark rivers in their necks,
chests, legs. Octavio was dragged outside
and executed near a spill of bougainvillea
that darkened when the tank
clattered forward, shadowing
the magenta blossoms, then rolled
over Octavio's body.
They couldn't kill him enough

When the guardsmen left,
the people came with white sheets, whispering
"Did you know his last two questions?"

Each year the people come to Octavio's church,
years after a peace that lets them starve.
They sing "When the poor believe in the poor
we will be able to sing freedom."
It is the only answer they have.

MARJORIE TUITE

MARJORIE TUITE grew up on New York's west side. As a young Dominican Sister, she was assigned to be principal of an all-boys Catholic high school in Harlem. Margie marched at Selma, took the "urban plunge" with the Ecumenical Center and Alinsky organizers in Chicago, trained organizers from the Bronx to Mississippi, and worked with farm worker communities in the Southwest and Michigan. In 1965, she co-founded the National Assembly of Religious Women. A charismatic proponent for social justice and an Irish wit, she was much in demand on the speaker's circuit.

By 1983, she'd become Nicaragua's most outspoken U.S. clerical advocate. On International Women's Day 1986, two thousand Nicaraguan women stood with lighted candles in the village of Esteli, chanting, "Reverenda Margie! Viva!" Two months after returning from her last visit to Nicaragua, she died of cancer. She requested that her ashes be buried in Nicaragua—a request her Dominican order reluctantly granted. Sandinista women paid her their highest honor by burying her in the Cemetery of Heroes and Martyrs.

LAST DESIRE

Because here a final ash has joined the assault.
　　　　　　　　—Ernesto Cardenal, "The Deserted City"

A thin New York rain
on your coffin.
The Dominicans follow,
forty years of catching up.
So you are still, a last ride across
Manhattan's black mirror streets.
Ada Maria pokes a fist
into the weeping air,
shouting your name,
and we all cry *Presente!*
again and again
until the hearse,
like a low-rider chariot,
carries you to fire.
One consummation before the freeing.
Then, sister, you are
light as breath,
and can fall, as you wished,
on Nicaragua's soil
to lie in the grainy arms
of a thousand mothers,
the holy embrace of martyrs,
with Louisa Amanda Espinosa, with Sandino.
A gringa, a nun,
dug into an earth
that hums beneath banana trees,
under the almond groves,
below Lake Managua's floating white herons,
harmonizing with the frog
songs of the river:
everything lives,

everything lives.
Oh, you, who never rested,
rest now in the dust
of mango groves.

Secundino says your solidarity was
clear as blue sweet water lagoons
because you were never
too tired for El Pueblo,
for las hermanas, for
the bag ladies, for the folks.
But I think you were
too tired, destructively tired,
tired almost to incomprehension.
But then I'd see you
drag that tiredness
one more step.
You'd move up to the line,
and one exquisite, seemingly
last time, you'd step over it.
Hurrah! She did it again! Viva!

So Marjorie, adelante.
Right now
we are stepping up
to their lines.
Watch us.

RICARDO MELARA

RICARDO MELARA was one of El Salvador's leading painters. Affiliated with the Farabundo Marti National Liberation Front (FMLN), he left the country at the end of the 1970s. Settling in Chicago, he organized a chapter of the Committee in Solidarity with the Salvadoran People and married a North American whose father had been a member of the Abraham Lincoln Brigade and had fought in Spain with the anti-fascist Republicans against Franco. Working full time at odd jobs and ceaselessly organizing both Salvadorans and North Americans to work for the end of the war in El Salvador, he nevertheless always found time to paint

In 1982, Melara was shot and killed by a Guatemalan—not in a war zone in El Salvador but on the west side of Chicago. The following poem is addressed to Melara's daughter, Maya.

THE ARTIST'S DAUGHTER

for Maya

1982

Always your father's memory,
a bravery you will not salute.
Your exiled father's unfinished revolution,
where blue volcanoes wait out the century,
impassive as stone lions, exquisite in
jacaranda trees with their tangle of magenta.

"Which is the dream, Papi?" you asked, at five years,
watching him paint in a land of silver corn,
skies whirling with alabaster doves,
floating ruby fish, ocher corpses, vultures;
then high above the mountains, mango groves,
a valley of scarlet carnations sweeping before a cemetery
of crosses, black-veiled peasants.
In the center is Abuelita,
her peasant face a wrinkled cloth.
The coal black eyes
defy you, defy your despair.

1999

Now the painting sits in your mother's dust-filled cabinet,
calling: *finish this, finish this,* as if it were
a revolution that could end well.
"Stay angry," your mother says.
In a dream Papi returns.
"Paint, Maya," he says, "turn sorrow to rain, frogs,
butterflies, fields of melons and maize;
let justice wear sandals of beauty,
walk the road made by every child,
peasant, and priest who died for her,
those who dance above the volcanoes,

confident and sinless.
"Paint that," Papi says.

But you refuse art school, refuse to travel to El Salvador.
You are an American girl. You wear black leather and purple
nail polish and play the Gypsy Kings over and over.
At seventeen, you dream you are five accompanying
Papi in his basement studio. His shirt and jeans
are stained turquoise, lavender and ivory,
his chestnut hands smeared canary yellow
from the suns he paints again and again.
"Why did they kill Grandma … And her burros
and chickens, Papi? Why did they cut them?"
"Look, Maya," he answers in the dream, sketching in a burro
and chickens that float above the village rooftops. "Nothing
dies," he says. "Nothing."

The next day you lay out his brushes,
then paint a burro trudging through a corn field.
Above Izalco you paint three suns,
your hands bright with their spill.

JUAN GERARDI CONDERA

JUAN GERARDI CONDERA was Bishop of the El Quiche diocese in the Guatemalan Highlands during the height of the wars against the Mayan populations in the early 1980s. So many catechists and priests were killed by the Guatemalan army that Gerardi took the unprecedented action of closing the diocese. The necessity of that action almost broke him.

It was his memory of this event that motivated Monsignor Gerardi to initiate the Recovery of Historic Memory (REMHI) project, which was completed in 1998. Over a two-year period, almost seven thousand people, mostly Mayan, reported what had occurred in their villages during the 1980s. The report, titled *Guatemala Nunca Más,* was intended to reveal the truth of the army's systematic elimination of Mayan populations and to begin to heal the deep wounds of those who carried the secrets of persecution, torture, and assassination. REMHI gave voice to those silenced by a war of terror.

REMHI investigators found that government forces were responsible for seventy-nine percent of the killings during this period, the guerrillas for nine percent.

On April 24, 1998, two days after the report was made public, Gerardi was killed, his head smashed in by concrete slabs. He was beaten so viciously that he could only be identified by his Bishop's ring. His friend, Father Ricardo Falla, said: "Archbishop Romero was killed with a bullet to the heart, as if to kill the love and passion that drove people to struggle. Gerardi was killed by someone who smashed his brain, as if they were trying to wipe out his memory." Forty-eight hours before he was murdered, Gerardi had publicly presented the REMHI report to the Mayan nations, saying, "We want to build a country different than the one we have now. For that reason, we are recovering the memory of our people. This path has been, and continues to be, full of risks, but the construction of God's Reign has risks and can only be built by those that have the strength to confront those risks."

GUATEMALA, NUNCA MÁS

I am the most gigantic of the dead who will never close his eyes
until I see you saved.

—Julia de Burgos

The Bishop speaks into a blind wind
that stabs its knife bone deep.
Here, in the altiplano, he hears Mayan children,
ghosts singing in the rocks.
"What is a shepherd?" he asks the dead.
He knows one thing: seminary dictums
are parrots repeating a parrot's gospel.
The Bishop pulls back, the way a flower
rises up in the hands of the wind.
"What is a shepherd here
in El Quiche?" he asks no one, recounting
the month's murders.

He closes down the diocese of El Quiche
as if it were a condemned building, because the church
he believed would protect them is marked, quemada.
What can he ask the nuncio
who sips wine with bishops?
"Brother, will you come here
where the dust is caked
with dark clots the color of sherry?"

Alone, he seeks the people,
wants cornfields without
a subterrain of skeletons,
wants a church with the imagination
of ordinary peasants.

Years after the dead covered the highlands
with a tattoo of Mayan bones,

years after Bishop Juan Gerardi can do
little more than cry, repeating
"Let me stay with you, my suffering friend,"
the Guatemalan earth answers back,
opening like a body to tell of the Maya in the 1980s:
the moist sack of earth with its trove of bones.

"Dig here," the Bishop says, "dig here."
The terrible witness of ribs, bashed skulls,
tiny femurs, and the frail wings of shoulder blades
speak of the Kabiles.

In the nineties, like a rain seen across a field,
survivors come down from the mountains to testify
because a Bishop who thought he was useless, asked them,
a Bishop who gives back to them their words,
a terrible witness of fire in a book that opened
the last door of the blackened house.
It is a book written by peasants whose
words tear open windows in the sealed walls.
"This path," the Bishop says, "is full of risks."

His last.

RUTILIO GRANDE

RUTILIO GRANDE, the son of peasants and the first priest killed in El Salvador's war, returned to the Aguilares region, where he grew up, to work with peasant farmers in the 1970s. He formed comunidades de base, or base Christian communities, in which he asked the peasants to teach him the meaning of the Gospel. Grande said that the Gospel as interpreted by peasants, whose children often die of malnutrition before they reach the age of four, is a radical text. It is the story of the liberation of the poor, the enslaved, the exiled. Such a living faith allows the peasants to reclaim their dignity.

"It is not right," they told Grande, "that landowners make us feed their dogs better food than we can feed our children." So they set about to organize a farm cooperative. That's when the big landowners and their defenders, the military, sent paramilitary groups to Aguilares to prevent farm workers from organizing.

A timid man, who was insecure about his vocation in a community of religious scholars, Grande blossomed in the midst of the campesinos he loved and trusted. As the numbers of catechists tortured and executed by the military increased, the Jesuit priest's public defense of peasant rights intensified. A month before he was killed, Grande gave this public homily, knowing that his words were being taped:

> Very soon the Bible and Gospel won't be allowed to cross our borders. We'll only get the bindings, because all the pages are subversive. I think if Jesus himself came across the border at Chalatenango, they wouldn't let him in. There are those in our brotherhood who would prefer a buried Christ, a dummy to carry through the streets in processions, a Christ with a muzzle in his mouth.... They do not want a God who will question us and trouble our consciences.... Some would rather have a God in the clouds, not Jesus of Nazareth who asks for lives lived in service to establishing a just order, the uplifting of the wretched, the values of the Gospel. It is dangerous to be a Christian.... It is almost illegal to be Catholic where the very preaching of the Gospel is subversive.

This sermon did not go unnoticed. Within weeks, on March 12, 1977, Rutilio Grande, accompanied by an old man, Don Manuel, and a young altar boy, Rutilio Lemus, traveled the road from Aguilares to El Paisnal, the town where Grande grew up, in order to offer mass to the villagers. Halfway there, the three were ambushed and killed.

BAGGAGE

I left carrying my father's words
packed in baggage too heavy to lift.
At seminary I stuffed a pack
with philosophy, theology, holiness.

My parishioners asked
for everything except what I'd packed.

Then I went to Aguilares where
no one has anything to pack.
The peasants are patient. When my bags
are empty, they ask me to tell them about the Bible.
But I, who have nothing to give,
ask them to tell me what the Gospel means.

Maria says, "I think we are the mustard seed,
because we are small and overlooked,
but we believe in the earth and
we believe in each other. So you see, Padre,
according to us, we are a beautiful tree,
a ceiba tree with roots profunda."

OSTMARO CACERES was killed in El Salvador in 1982. I met his father, Señor Caceres, when a Salvadoran pastoral worker offered to take us into the Aguilares region after the military command headquarters denied us permission to enter the countryside. Our guide took a campesino route, leading us a day through the countryside, circumventing military checkpoints.

Father Rutilio Grande had been slain in the Aguilares region in 1977. Following Grande's assassination, the military had executed two hundred members of the Christian base communities there because they considered agricultural cooperatives to be subversive. Any priest—like the newly ordained Caceres—who attempted to serve these communities was automatically targeted by the military.

A FATHER'S MEMORY

The road from El Barrillo
to Aguacayo parts a river,
green plumes of trees
fall over clay banks
where peasants dug
bomb shelters in '81 and '82.
At the gnarled Anono trees,
bent forward like choir monks,
we turn off.

In front of the priest's house,
the old man touches my arm, whispers:

> "They came through both doors,
> He was not ordained a month.
> I warned him."

Torogoses whistle and soar
above the caved roof where wisteria
spills violet over
a wall pocked
with bullet holes.
A balm of leaves
pours through the caved roof.
From habit the old man
pulls off his sombrero,
enters the casita.
He touches a dusty shelf
bleached gray.
Silence holds everything
awash in the alabaster light.

> "On his ordination day
> everything was white.

We ate pupusas,
drank guaro.
A marimba played.
I kissed my boy's hands.
Then he said,
'If they come, Papa,
keep this blessing.
Denounce me.'"

In the predawn hours of November 16, 1989, thirty soldiers from the elite Atlacatl Battalion entered the Jesuit University of Central America in San Salvador, dragged six Jesuits from their beds, and shot them in the head at point-blank range. The Jesuits' housekeeper, Elba Ramos, and her daughter, Celina, were also shot. The murders were witnessed by Lucia Barrera de Cerna, who had hidden herself from the soldiers.

Colonel Benavides and two lieutenants were convicted of the murders and incarcerated. They have since been released. Church officials insisted that the order to assassinate the Jesuits could only have come from the military high command as part of a military operation known as the Jakarta Plan. According to the Archbishop of El Salvador, Arturo Rivera y Damas,

> *Bishop Rosa Chavez and I could have died, too, on that night. Our names were listed in the Jakarta Plan, which sought the physical elimination of all of us who denounce human rights violations and the system of injustice here in El Salvador.*

In 1993, the United Nations Truth Commission Report for El Salvador determined that the assassinations of the six Jesuits and two women were planned and executed by the Salvadoran military. Additionally, the Truth Commission raised questions about the United States' complicity in the Salvadoran military's crimes—because the U.S government sent six billion dollars in aid to the Salvadoran government during the war and because the U.S. military trained the Salvadoran military. The Atlacatl Brigade, for example, which had been trained at the School of the Americas in Fort Benning, Georgia, was responsible for the deaths of over 200 people at Calabozo in 1982, 118 people in Copapayo in 1983, 68 people in Los Llanitos in 1984, and 50 people at the Gualsinga River in 1984, in addition to the eight people killed at the Jesuit University of Central America in 1989.

The Latin phrase *ad sum* means, "I am here." It is the answer each young deacon speaks when he is called for priestly ordination by a bishop.

AD SUM

*for six Jesuits and their housekeepers assassinated in El Salvador,
November 16, 1989*

Three a.m. Night unclenches
the day's fist of heat,
cools the campus lawn.
Colonel Benavides orders thirty-five men
through the university gate.
They crush carnations, tear
ground ivy. Dew glistens
on their black boots.
A brush of pine colognes
their wrists, their ankles.
The Atlacatl brigade runs
toward the priests' compound,
shadows in the moonfall.
Inside, a thread of breath
pulls the sleeper's muscles.
Colonel Benavides turns away.
Nothing could have been done,
he says, stroking his jaw.

     Lucia Barrera de Cerna
Lucia wakes to drills of gunfire jack-
hammering the air, slamming
into adobe walls, poles, sheds,
the barrio itself a body, shattering.
She knows this ending,
already imagines each convulsive
jolt of the priests' bodies.
She must witness, be pulled
to the furnace's open door.
Oh, Padres, this I can do.

    President Alfredo Cristiani
The President twists under
damp white sheets, wrestling
a presence that pins
each move. The winner speaks:
"Expect no witnesses."
The moon will not tell.
If it does, there are solutions.
If the moon were a lily,
it could be trampled in the dark earth;
or if, say, a horse prancing
the starry fields,
it could be brought down,
hit clean between the eyes,
its huge flanks pumping.
Sleeper, dream on.

    Celina Ramos (Notes from the Dead)
Mama prays in the dark.
Monsignor stares from the photo
into her black eyes like a mirror
or some angel
who knows her
better than we do.
Monsignor this, Monsignor that.
Me, I watch her hands,
roll the dough,
pinch the crust
as if it were wafer.
Padre Amando Lopez teases: "Profesora."
But I don't know books.
What I know
is an intelligence of hands.

    The Jesuits
Lt. Espinosa calls each name,

orders them to lie face down.
Some are dragged;
others walk forward, answering
a call that has reached them
across years, oceans, the heave
of grave upon grave.
The answer: *Ad Sum*, spoken
on ordination day so many years before
as young deacons lying prostrate
on a church marble floor
drenched with incense, rose lupine,
young men who answered a God
who would escape their adulation
ingenious as Houdini handcuffed
in a trunk under water—
a God who reappears as a campesina,
hungry and exhausted,
with a child on her hip,
a God of the despised,
of peasants, of women.

Prostrate again, the Jesuits lie against an earth,
heavy with a mulch of seeds and crushed flowers.
"Bishop, Lieutenant, my people,
Ad sum. I am here."
Faithful despite betrayal
by Christian nations
that watched stranglers' hands
at the throats of children,
heard their screams daily for
ten years and did nothing.

Oh, how demanding the light
has been, knifing its cold shaft
into the heart's dumb secrets,
touching the dark floor where

El Mozote, Rio Lempa, and Sumpul
lie torn open.

The executioners—Sergeant Avalos,
(nicknamed "Satan") and
Private Oscar Amaya—step forward,
lift AK 47s into firing position.
One last voice is heard.
It is "Nacho" Martin-Baro.
He does not beg. Shouts
last judgment: *This is barbaric!*
Nothing more.
Close range AK 47s split craniums
fragile as porcelain.
As if ideas were muscle,
gristle, bone, meat,
as if an eternity of desire will end with this.

In the morning soldiers march
past the Bishop's residence, shouting:
"We'll go on killing communists.
Ellacuria and Martin-Baro have already fallen."
A fifteen-year-old cups his hands to his mouth,
checks for a running path, then shouts back:
"Risen! Ellacuria and Martin-Baro have already risen!"

Joaquin Lopez y Lopez
    Ad Sum.
Ignacio Ellacuria
    Ad Sum.
Amando Lopez
    Ad Sum.
Elba Ramos
    Ad Sum.

Celina Ramos
> *Ad Sum.*

Segundo Montes
> *Ad Sum.*

Juan Ramon Moreno
> *Ad Sum.*

Ignacio Martin-Baro
> *Ad Sum.*

THE PEASANT POEMS

LUPE

LUPE is a grandmother who belongs to the Panchimilama repopulation village, which lies on a valley floor, one hour's walk straight down a mountain. The repopulation movement of El Salvador has been referred to as the Salvadoran's "Salt March" because thousands of campesinos who'd spent eight years in Honduran refugee camps collectively decided to walk back to their ancestral lands with seed and children in hand in the midst of a war, demanding peace and a chance to plant once again.

It is 1988. Panchimilama is very tense. Lutheran church workers have been denied access to the camp, the army has blocked seed and medicine shipments, and two campesinos have been killed and one international worker has been injured by grenade explosions.

Lupe says the army wants to intimidate the people into leaving. The Panchimilama community has planted and harvested five crops, they've built a health clinic, formed a women's sewing collective, and organized a baby chick and collective milk feeding project.

Lupe says, "We've marked the land."

I WILL SING

Wary of gringos,
she does not join
the mothers who greet us
as wheat sun falls through
a grey rope of smoke and dust.
Where she kneads corn dough,
calla lilies of light
have fallen onto the river of her arms,
across the grinding stone
her father made.

She came from Tenancingo.

> "Orejas listened in our meetings.
> My neighbor was taken …
> My town was full of birds—"

until the bombs split it,
the tongues of church bells
smashing back and forth,
a bray of burros high-pitched,
children crouched on the hip-bone
of a village ridge, waiting.

After Tenancingo three years
of dust, mud, rats in corn bins.

> "Maybe in Tenancingo the birds
> returned with the people.
> Not me, not with all those ghosts."

Late sun rolls off
rows of fat tortillas
she's stacked ten high.

She whispers to us:

>"They killed my husband, sister, mother.
>I don't like to remember
>because there is a hole inside
>nothing can fill."

She stops, pulling back.

>"Comunidad transforms suffering."

Stunned, I ask her to repeat *transform*
for us whose children
are without worms,
who lay down without listening
for the snap of jack boots
in the underbrush.

>"I always wanted to live in a
>community with guitars.
>Even though I'm an old woman,
>I won't become crazy
>to my children,
>let sadness win.
>I will sing."

THE FARABUNDO MARTI NATIONAL LIBERATION FRONT

For twelve years, the Farabundo Marti National Liberation Front (FMLN) fought a low-intensity war with the U.S.-backed Salvadoran military. When, after a long stalemate, the peace accords were signed in 1991, the FMLN commander, Joaquin Villalobos, did not press strongly for land reform because he believed that the ruling party, ARENA, which was dominated by the military and rich landowners, would refuse to sign the accords. Many of the peasants felt betrayed by the FMLN's failure to win land reform, because that was the key reason the war had been fought in the first place.

The FMLN, or Frente (Front) for short, was made up of teenagers, women, peasants, workers, students, and intellectuals. Thousands of the guerrillas died fighting for the liberation of the poor majority—a liberation that could only be complete with true land reform. This poem is dedicated to those anonymous guerrillas who did not count their lives more important than the people they fought for and who obeyed the orders of their leaders who later failed them.

The occasion of this poem was a fiesta in the honor of Saint Martha, the patron saint of the village of Santa Marta. Santa Marta lies near a river at the Honduran border, where hundreds of fleeing Salvadorans attempted to escape the Salvadoran military in 1981. The Honduran military blocked the river until the Salvadoran military could arrive. On March 18, 1981, hundreds of women, children, and old men were massacred. When we visited Santa Marta in 1988, it was being protected by members of the Frente, who, on the night of the celebration, surround the village with guards and permit guerrillas with relatives in the village to take part in the festivities.

THE FRENTE

Unless you have come to give
your heart and mind,
your coming
will be your going....
Here you must be the last to sleep,
the last to keep,
the last to eat,
the first to die.

—FMLN guerrilla poem

That night in Santa Marta the muchachos
sneak through a cane field,
hyenas who chuckle under stars' silver daggers,
the saint's celebration their holy shield.

We are swaying to a ranchera lilt, dipping beneath
a straw canopy, when they step to the floor.
Astonished, I whisper in your ear *The Frente! The Frente!*
as if the revolution had flung wide its secret door.

Suddenly they are dancing with novias, wives,
women who to them are a muted choir.
Thick-booted men whirl in candlelight, their faces,
hands, gold with sweat, every move waking desire.

I can't take my eyes off them—their stoic silence:
fathers, sons, each committed to his terrible turn.
They walk thirty miles a day, a ragged army living on beans,
their bones and blood a gift that will burn

luminous as the Ocote torch, years from now.
Tonight, their sentinels hand off weapons,
then enter the dance near tears, pulling lovers close—
boys who will face the hour of deceptions.

Near dawn we watch them fade into shadow, rustling
corn stalks. Then silence. Their distant boots light
on the volcano's dark stairs. War will remove
their shining eyes, the beauty of this night.

The FMLN is an army of poets who believe, like Roque Dalton,
that poems are bread. But bread some
steal from any mouth, which their leaders do,
leaving them hungry, landless in the peace deal.

Those somber guerrillas danced toward the morning star.
They were the last to sleep or eat, the last to ask why.
Men and women whose lives were poems they ate
like bread. They were the first to die.

THE WOUNDED

In an archdiocesan refugee camp outside San Salvador, wounded combatants of the Farabundo Marti National Liberation Front (FMLN) waited under the protection of the Salvadoran Church for safe accompaniment to medical centers in Europe. Most suffered wounds or impairments that required specialized medical technology or skill.

LISIADOS

"Lisiados." The camp nurse
barely moves her lips,
edges us past their barracks.
Candlelight flickers
where they play checkers,
pouring strong guaro down
dark throats, laughing.
A boy without a jaw strokes
a cat, his smile crooked.

In dreams they gather
arms, legs, hands,
missing parts of a puzzle
their bodies cannot remember.
There are screams:
parrots, a man's sob.
Night air opens the muffled voice,
allows sorrow to speak,
touches sleeping senses
with the scent of volcano flowers,
their mountain, Guazapa,
where they vaulted from conacaste trees,
acrobats in the trustworthy air.

ESTELA

ESTELA was an FMLN radio operator for six years of the war. When the Peace Accords were signed in El Salvador, she expected that she, like many guerrillas, would be supported by the FMLN, which had gained some initial political power. But it didn't happen. She struggled to reclaim her relationship with a child she hadn't seen until he was six, and to support her family in a post-war economy that left the poor in more desperate financial condition than before the war.

THE PUMA

I am the puma walking
through stars on the volcano.
I wear men's clothes, a bandanna,
boots, an M16 on my shoulder.

Starving generations have carried me
to this volcano.
When breathless soldiers reach our camp,
pirouetting left, then right,
trigger fingers throbbing,
they find coals, a cane lean-to,
the murmur of pine boughs,
as we leap through
a green door peasants close.
No jefe, no guerrillas vinieron aqui.

When my baby is born,
I christen him Oscar,
oil his black curls,
kiss his hands, feet.

I give life in this dying revolution.
I am the scripture my compañeros
have never read.

Good-bye, hijo, I say.
Your grandmother will sing
to you until I return,
or don't.

Now, I move through the canefields,
a milky stain on my undershirt.
I grasp my rifle, my other hand
touches the dew-soaked darkness

seeking a cradle to rock.
Fists of flame, sudden as a blow torch,
burst behind us.

Six years of carrying a radio
as if it were a zensontle bird
that could fly above mortar,
singing: *Danger, danger.*
If I fall, sing on, pajarito
in my compas' hands.

Six years of prowling.
Six years of Commandante Villalobos
saying: "See how they fear us."
Six years of corpses.
Six years of peasants dying to protect us.
Six years of mud and bitter coffee.

ROMERO'S ANNIVERSARY PROCESSION

*If I am killed, let my blood be as seeds of liberty for this suffering
people.*

—Oscar Romero, Archbishop of San Salvador

Every March, thousands of Salvadorans process through the streets of San
Salvador to the cathedral where Monsignor Romero is buried to commem-
orate the anniversary of his death. During the war, armed soldiers would
flank the streets during the procession. To have a picture of Romero in your
home branded you a subversive.

Birds fly in and out of the cathedral, which Romero refused to reno-
vate, insisting that the Church's money belonged to the poor, since they, not
the building, were the Church.

ANNIVERSARY

March 24

They step, step into the street,
carrying Romero's words
on torn sheet banners:
"I don't believe in death
without resurrection.
If they kill me, I will
rise in the Salvadoran people."
Thousands march in the footsteps of ghosts.
In each fist, sprigs of fern,
a spray of white laurel.

A line of mothers in white bandannas,
black dresses, plastic sandals passes.
As if handing out bread
the mothers of the disappeared,
the murdered, the tortured,
pass with a blessing:
Receive the body of my daughter,
my son, broken for you.

I am greeting Luisa and Paco,
catechists from El Barrillo,
who've walked since daybreak,
avoiding army checkpoints.
The Tres Ceibas comunidad tracked over
the belly of moonlit fields,
carrying children, sacks of tortillas,
mangoes, armloads of Flor de Hizote
with their milky stalks.
They've come toward the city,
their approach a whisper of maize,
cocoa, bones, skulls.

PEASANT TEACHERS

In the conflict zones like Guazapa, the peasants educated their children even in the refugee camps, constructing cane-stalk or tree-shaded classrooms in the open air. Since the end of the war, the peasant teachers have sought to be officially certified by the government to teach in the schools. But ARENA party members have told the peasant teachers that they can only be certified if they complete a program of coursework at the university in San Salvador. Unfortunately, these "barefoot teachers" can afford neither the seventy-five-cent bus ride to and from the capital each weekend nor a lost weekend of work on the land. Without certification they receive no salary for their teaching. Still, the peasant teachers continue to teach, without salaries, in the "new" El Salvador.

POPULAR EDUCATION

The teacher, Marie Isabel, walks toward the milpa
carrying a basket of pupusas and salt fish.
Outside Suchitoto they are walking
in from Guazapa, singing
Dale! Salvadorans! Dale!
Who are these frail peasants who
come from earthen buzones
where they hid from battalions trampling
through the ash of squash and sorghum fields?

Marie Isabel is not interested in the past
only this bread and tetracycline she
distributes like sacraments.

The sandaled teachers walk in
loping strides, shy and grinning.
These intellectuals of the campo
forge knowledge on the anvil
of paper and pen.
They are the text that says:
I am hungry.
I am not dead.
I am coming.

THE SERGEANT

When we tried to enter a conflict zone in Chalatenango, Sergeant Martinez tore up the salvo-cunductos, or safe conduct passes, we had waited for days to receive. We spent an entire day negotiating with the sergeant, to no avail. At sundown, we began to hear the sporadic exchange of gunfire outside the town. Nervous, we left the Cuartel (army headquarters and barracks) and spent the night sleeping in hammocks in a school courtyard, offered to us by a local priest.

Sergeant Martinez told us that, when he was a young recruit in 1980, his unit had attacked peasants fleeing across the Sumpul River. Six hundred refugees—mostly women, children, and old men—were massacred at Rio Sumpul.

WAITING FOR PASSES

Our safe conduct passes lay
behind the sergeant's desk. Hopeless.
Corinna, he calls me, rolling
the r's like a radio announcer.
Corinna, he repeats familiarly,
reading the passport name I never use.

The Cuartel is a fortress of buildings
hunched behind plump sandbags
piled up like dead animals.
Inside, men with black mustaches
and black mirror glasses
parade past lines of Jeep Cherokees
with smoked dark windows.
The sergeant produces a single white gardenia,
which he offers, arrogant and gallant.
"Para la poesia," his eyes slits.
He'd read *Profession? Writer,*
and guessed I was a poet.

We wait two hours
to deliver seed, medicines to campesinos.
"Fijate, for your own protection,
I cannot permit you
on the road to Guarjila.
Terrorists ahead," he shrugs.
Because of the absurd gardenia,
I think he believes this lie.
We insist. Amused, his mustache lifts slightly.

But it is the sergeant
who's not considered the odds.
Distant rattles of firepower
burst intermittently under a
silver-hammered moon.

They surround you, sergeant,
dark cinnamon men with your
black eyes, women of mud
and oily bandannas.
They slip through green walls
in the mountain, move like iguanas
through the starry groves,
a fragrance of mangoes
lingers on their hands.
They have nothing to lose, sergeant,
nothing.

"Corinna, why do your
people bring food to these farmers?"
The sergeant does not say
the word *subversive*.
He thinks gringos know nothing.
"I am a Christian," he says,
as if it explained something.

But the sergeant does not remember
the morning, does not remember 7 a.m.
when eleven-year-old Jose,
who stepped on a mine,
lay in the truck, bleeding in his
mother's lap, bloody fingerprints
on the permit she hands the sergeant,
the child's blanket stiff with blood.
The sergeant does not remember
calculating how long it would take
to bleed away this childhood.
"They won't make it past
Suchitoto," he'd said.

He only remembers the first time of blood,
the river seven years before,

when he was a boy with a gun,
how he ate mangoes while they marched
through the corpses.
He ate mangoes for days after Rio Sumpul.

ANA MARIA'S BABY

ANA MARIA is a twenty-six-year-old mother who lives in Chalatenango. Her daughter was born in an underground shelter, or tatu, during the war.

TATU

In the tunnel
we cannot see the grey sky,
where bombers whine.
Then, a sickening pause,
thud. The dirt walls rattle, loosen
grit into our eyes and noses.
A shaft of light steadies
where the sifting dust rolls.
And there, in the fetid air,
a mother delivers an olive baby.
The tiny cries break our terrified silence,
loosening to one pure breath.

When we climb into the smoking silence,
December has spilled a gourd of stars
over the milpa.
The aftermath of birth is the history
of one exhaustion, one triumph.
The mother,with her infant, runs breathless
through the milky fields,
well ahead of the patrols.
We cannot take our eyes off her,
wanting to understand
what she is giving,
why she is not
the saviour of the world.

CONGREGATION OF MOTHERS

A campesina named Benancia describes the Congregation of Mothers' effect on the devastated communities in the eastern war zones as "the yeast that lifted" the whole Morazan community. When she refers to "all that happened in the 1980s" in the testimony below, she is speaking about the destruction of the village of El Mozote. The Salvadoran air force bombed El Mozote for several hours, killing all but one person in the village. One thousand people perished. All of the people in the region east of the Torola River were so terrified by this act of scorched-earth terrorism that they desisted from resistance of virtually any kind. Even the prayer and bible reflection groups in the base Christian communities stopped meeting, for fear of being labeled subversivos. This response was, of course, the military's objective. After months of isolation and fear, the Congregation of Mothers, who had been holding secret scripture reflection meetings, decided to break the grip of terror by risking their lives to confront Colonel Vargas at his army post just across the Torola River.

When the Congregation of Mothers began, the atmosphere of repression was still very present. All that happened in the 1980s had been committed so that the people would not come together, so that they would be afraid to hold any type of meeting.... Because the men were more persecuted by the armed forces, they were afraid to get involved in doing anything for the community.... But the women, by means of their actions, spoke to the men, telling them that united it was possible to overcome oppression.... As the women began to confront the armed forces and demand their rights, the men began to discover that they too could do something in their communities.

I came to admire these women—their unity and their willingness to stand up to repression, which, in turned, caused the men to stand up.... The Congregation of Mothers was like a yeast that lifted the whole community.

MORAZAN LIFTED

After El Mozote, they
shut frail doors
against each other,
against memory, or
against the smallest act of courtesy
that might embrace them,
might invite voices.
Because then they'd come
for the children,
for names,
and the mothers would
save the children,
paying with their sex
or naming a campesino
they cherished.

So they stayed behind doors
saturated with the scent
of lemons and mint,
under roofs of baked mud,
bone-white when the moon
fell through the pacun trees.
In the years of doors,
Paco's boy died of measles,
Luisa's from hunger,
fourteen from diarrhea,
eleven from pneumonia.
No medicines, no seed
could pass the checkpoint
at San Francisco de Gotera
where Colonel Vargas called
El Mozote a triumph.

Vargas' battalion: each face eerily
smeared with black jungle paint,
country boys appointed with boots
no peasant could afford,
clips of ammo, M16s
slung on their shoulders.
The mothers: their memories,
their rage, and the doors of Morazan.
Doors they'd open,
and a sigh of light would
brush everything,
threatening to remember
the time before closed doors
when they were girls
and the plaza filled with
the music of rancheras,
a bullfrog chonchona bass
singing to the night.

So they blessed each other and
sent five mothers who would pass
Vargas' checkpoint, walk
to the city, persuade the Bishop
to send four truckloads of food.

When they returned,
Vargas called them whores,
ordered the trucks back.
In that moment Matilde's voice,
her old voice, returned:
"Colonel, without this food
our babies will die.
So we may as well die, too."
The mothers blocked the trucks path.
Vargas said, "Putas!"—and waited.
The mothers waited. For days.

After three dawns a soldier flagged
the trucks forward. Spools of sunlight
unraveled over muscled foothills, lay
dark rose threads on the Torola River.
Behind the trucks,
a trail of mothers advanced
into that sepia light—
women who desired the eyes
of their people, their shyness,
that moment to return
the looted earth's
maize, rice, and seed,
that moment without sorrow,
stepping into the village
filling with applause.

COTTON PICKERS OF CHINANDEGA

Outside Chinandega, Nicaragua, a small school and infant care center built by the AMNLAE, a national women's organization, sits in the middle of a cotton field. When we visit the center in 1983, we watch the children of the cotton pickers recite the alphabet, count numbers, and then roar the national anthem, shouting *Viva!* at the end loudly enough to wake the sleeping babies in the next room. Before the revolution, the mothers would place their babies near them in the fields. Because there were no trees for hammocks or shade, the mothers would cover the babies with sheets. But, while they could protect them from the sun, they could not protect them from bugs or snakes.

WORKING THE LAND

Here on the bin floor of border mountains
that once rolled fields of orange groves
as far as Leon, I work a land
unable to remember its own gilded orchards—
that time before Somoza's growers
leveled all to the dust of cotton fields.
When the campo whispers, and our mountains
slip dawn on purple shoulders,
I arise with the silent women.
Before daybreak spills the last
morning star from Nicaragua's violet sky,
before Bluefields fishermen prepare nets,
before newsboys scuffle barefoot
into Esteli's chalky streets,
before the women open Market Oriental,
a revival tent flooding with light,
before lassoes of sunlight
pull Managua cement workers
onto rickety buses,
before my sleeping compañero,
a braid of muscle and dreams, awakens,
we, the mothers of Chinandega,
gather into that crack of opening light.

Hours before searing sun
turns the fields
to a white whistle of heat,
we begin our work.

DISPLACED PEOPLE

The Salvadoran coastal region of Usulatan was a conflict zone. Los desplazados—the displaced people—had no homes, not even cane shacks, because they had to move frequently to avoid detection by gun-ship planes. In 1985, a helicopter mounted with a machine gun turret fired upon a band of their community doing field work.

WAR ZONE

I

This far inland, fear
is common as ceiba trees,
endurance unexceptional
as the mustard dust
choking our van.
From across the field
a reflection of peasants fly past
our van windows, impervious
as an olive grove,
as if their feet
were sown into the soil.
The Generals call campesinos "the sea."
General Blandon wants the sea
drained of its stubbornness,
wants a dead sea,
bloated fish floating up
from the depths, staring
with blind nickel eyes
into indigo nothingness.

Further on we wheel past blue
muscled mountains.
Now the road sign reads
EL PLAYON, the human dump
where in '81 and '82 hooked fish
gulped their last breaths,
bleeding together in a tangle of hooks,
a truckload of ruined bodies
thrown down the sides.

II

We cross a narrow railroad trestle
near the exploded Bridge of Gold
fallen into the Lempa River,
a set of gold teeth, still smiling.

Military patrols prowl
tight-knit and dull,
following bully-boy orders.
Ahead, the road folds into mud.
Suddenly, up from the river bed,
a wave of mothers appear, their
children with pear-shaped stomachs
full of worms. The refugees of Usulatan.
They arrange themselves under
leaves of ceiba and eucalyptus,
their only protection from
low-flying bombers,
clapping a welcome for
the "noble" Americans. We weep.

One guitar wails a ranchera.
Their voices are full in that dense emerald house.
Oh my friends, the song
winging through the arcs
of that forsaken woods
was a song of thanksgiving to
"God, who has accompanied us, always."

ACCOMPANIMENT

Tell me what I have lost
in your country, walking in
your sandal prints along

Guazapa's blue apron,
terrified to step beyond the circumference
of your determined path.

We cross scorched minefields, then cut
a swath through the blue tangle of cornstalks.
You, a dancer, in the killing fields.

Because you are familiar with loss,
I ask you this, Maria Teresa.
Because you have watched the gringas

come into this road of bones with sturdy boots
that outlast the peasant's thongs,
I ask you what I have left behind.

I know the obvious losses:
nostalgia for a history
received like a family heirloom,

a portfolio of immaculate plans.
I ran out of protection; my sorrow,
my imagination—both

failed. No distance from that dying baby
too weak for a last bawl,
a protest against pain, her odds.

When the mothers carry her pine coffin
towards the cemetery with its solemnity
of plastic flowers, rusted rosaries, white
crosses perched like a descent of blind doves,
I hear the immense ocean that separates me,
that will sweep me to my country's comfort

where I will never be safe again.